Contents

Extra-Silly Tales

Introduction

Welcome to *First Comprehension: Comics*! The 25 comic strips in this collection were developed to boost reading comprehension skills . . . and make kids chuckle. The easy-to-read pages include repetition, decodable and high-frequency words, predictable patterns, and picture clues to aid in fluency so children can focus on the meaning of what they read. Reproducible comprehension activities let children check their understanding by answering age-perfect questions, responding to true/false items, and drawing informative pictures.

The texts in each category—Friends and Family, Animal Adventures, and Extra-Silly Tales—increase in difficulty, giving you the flexibility to meet the needs of children at different ability levels. They are correlated with guided reading levels A–E. (See page 7 for the specific level of each story.) Each text is paired with a comprehension activity page that children complete to demonstrate their understanding of what they have read. The items include important skills, such as identifying main ideas and details, sequencing, making predictions and inferences, understanding cause and effect, and more.

You can use the texts and comprehension activities for whole-class, small group, or one-on-one comprehension instruction. The sample lesson plan (page 8) provides a framework for introducing and modeling reading in a meaningful context, as well as for after-reading discussion and completing the comprehension activities. The texts also work well as learning-center or take-home activities. Best of all, the activities support children in meeting the reading standards for Literary and Foundational Skills for grades K–2. (See Connecting to the Standards, page 9.)

How to Use

The texts and companion activity pages in this book are ideal for use as part of your instruction in comprehension. Research shows that comprehension instruction can help all readers, including emergent and struggling readers, improve comprehension by understanding, remembering, and communicating with others about what they read. Improved comprehension also creates greater enjoyment in reading, which leads to children wanting to read more!

Preparing to use these texts for comprehension instruction is as easy as 1, 2, 3! Simply make copies of a selected text and comprehension activity for each child, distribute the pages, then follow the sample lesson on page 8 to guide your instruction. You'll see that the sample lesson is very similar to an interactive read-aloud in which fluent, expressive reading is modeled while teaching the reading process in a meaningful context. The steps guide you to encourage higher levels of thinking and questioning that will help children develop understanding of the text, build vocabulary and background knowledge, and make connections to prior knowledge, self, and the world.

Teaching Tips

- Prior to the lesson, preview the text to become familiar with it.

- Identify any vocabulary that might need to be introduced.

- Enlarge the text page and display it so that everyone has a clear view of the text and illustrations.

- As you ask purposeful questions, remember that "why" and "how" questions prompt deeper thinking about the meaning of the text.

- Encourage children to ask questions and share their understanding of the text.

- Invite children to retell the story.

- Work with the whole class, small groups, or individuals to complete the comprehension page. Before children begin to fill in the page, read aloud each item and have children follow along. They can then go back and work on their own.
- As needed, model how to complete the short answer and true/false sections of the comprehension page.
- Allow children to dictate their responses to items on the comprehension page.

Learning Centers

Place copies of the desired text and comprehension pages in a folder. During their turn at the center, have children take a copy of each page and independently work through the text and comprehension activity. To make the activity self-checking, enlarge the answer key for the corresponding comprehension page and staple that page to the inside of the folder. When children complete the activity, they can check their responses by referring to the answer key.

Ways to Use the Texts

The texts and companion comprehension activities are ideal for the following:

- Whole-class instruction
- Small-group instruction
- One-on-one lesson
- Learning center activity
- Individual seatwork
- Take-home practice

Guided Reading Level

Correlated by a team of guided reading specialists.

Sample Lesson

Follow the steps below to provide comprehension instruction for the text of your choice.

1. Display a copy of the text page, making sure everyone can see it. Use sticky notes to cover each of the four panels on the page.

2. Point out and read the title. Ask: "What do you think this text will be about?" Encourage children to share their predictions.

3. Take a quick picture walk through the panels, but do not read the text. Reveal one panel at a time, starting with the first panel and ending with the last. This allows children to see the pictures in sequence so they can start constructing meaning.

4. Invite children to share what they know about the text topic, based on their predictions and the picture walk. This helps them relate to the text and sets the stage for making additional predictions and connections as the lesson continues. Also, introduce any unfamiliar or difficult vocabulary words from the text.

5. Read the text aloud. Use lots of expression, animation, and enthusiasm to really engage children. Pause to ask purposeful questions and check children's understanding of the text and pictures. Model a think-aloud process to encourage understanding and thinking beyond the text and to explore vocabulary. For example, "I wonder why the character did that"; "I think this word means _____ because _____"; and "That reminds me of _____." Invite children to share their own comments, questions, and observations during the read-aloud.

6. After reading, talk about the details and main points of the text. Invite children to share their understanding of the text.

7. Review the comprehension page with children before having them complete it. Encourage children to write their short answer responses in complete sentences and to refer to the text to check their work. Afterward, invite them to share and discuss their responses.

Connecting to the Standards

The lessons in this book support the College and Career Readiness Anchor Standards for Reading for students in grades K–12. These broad standards, which serve as the basis of many state standards, were developed to establish rigorous educational expectations with the goal of providing students nationwide with a quality education that prepares them for college and careers. The chart below details how the lessons align with specific reading standards for literary and informational texts for students in grades K through 2.

Foundational Skills

Print Concepts

- Demonstrate understanding of the organization and basic features of print.
- Follow words from left to right, top to bottom, and page by page.
- Recognize that spoken words are represented in written language by specific sequences of letters.
- Understand that words are separated by spaces in print.
- Recognize and name all upper- and lowercase letters of the alphabet.
- Recognize the distinguishing features of a sentence (e.g., first word, capitalization, ending punctuation).

Phonics and Word Recognition

- Know and apply grade-level phonics and word analysis skills in decoding words.
- Demonstrate basic knowledge of one-to-one letter-sound correspondences.
- Associate the long and short sounds with the common spellings for the five major vowels.
- Distinguish between similarly spelled words by identifying the sounds of the letters that differ.
- Decode regularly spelled one-syllable words.
- Know final -e and common vowel team conventions for representing long vowel sounds.
- Use knowledge that every syllable must have a vowel sound to determine the number of syllables in a printed word.
- Recognize and read grade-appropriate irregularly spelled words.

Fluency

- Read emergent-reader texts with purpose and understanding.
- Read grade-level text orally with accuracy, appropriate rate, and expression on successive readings.
- Use context to confirm or self-correct word recognition and understanding, rereading as necessary.

Literary Skills

Key Ideas and Details

- Ask and answer questions about key details in a text.
- Retell familiar stories, including key details.
- Identify characters, settings, and major events in a story.
- Describe characters, settings, and major events in a story, using key details.

Craft and Structure

- Ask and answer questions about unknown words in a text.
- Name the author and illustrator of a story and define the role of each in telling the story.
- Identify who is telling the story at various points in a text.

Integration of Knowledge and Ideas

- Describe the relationship between illustrations and the story in which they appear.
- Compare and contrast the adventures and experiences of characters in familiar stories.

Range of Reading and Level of Text Complexity

- Actively engage in group reading activities with purpose and understanding.

I Dress Up

1

2

3

4

WRITE!

1. What does the girl dress up as FIRST?

_____

- -

_____

- -

_____

2. What insect does the girl dress up as?

_____

_____

_____

- -

_____

SHADE!

1. The girl dresses up as a cat.

(TRUE)   (FALSE)

2. The girl dresses up as a dinosaur.

(TRUE)   (FALSE)

DRAW!

What do you like to dress up as?

Big Surprise

1

2

3

4

WRITE!

1. What do the friends bring to the party?

_____

- -

_____

_____

- -

_____

2. What happens at the end of the story?

_____

- -

_____

_____

- -

_____

SHADE!

1. One friend has a cake.

TRUE   FALSE

2. One friend has a flower.

TRUE   FALSE

DRAW!

How old is the girl? Draw a cake with that many candles.

Baby's Socks

1

Baby put the socks on his ears. What a sight!

2

Baby put the socks on his eyes. What a sight!

3

Baby put the socks on his hands. What a sight!

4

Baby put the socks on his feet. That is right!

WRITE!

1. What is Baby playing with?

_____

- -

_____

- -

_____

2. Is Baby silly? Why?

_____

- -

_____

_____

- -

_____

SHADE!

1. Baby is young.

TRUE   FALSE

2. Baby is old.

TRUE   FALSE

DRAW!

Where does Baby put his socks at the end of the story?

Hide-and-Seek Mouse

1

I can find my mouse. He is in the box!

2

I can find my mouse. He is in the mug!

3

I can find my mouse. He is in the book!

4

I cannot find my mouse. Where is he?

WRITE!

1. What game are the mouse and boy playing?

_____

_____

_____

_____

2. What is the FIRST place the mouse hides?

_____

_____

_____

SHADE!

1. The mouse hides in a bag.

(TRUE)   (FALSE)

2. The mouse hides in a mug.

(TRUE)   (FALSE)

DRAW!

What place does the mouse
NOT get found?

My Picture

1. Look at my picture. I just drew a pizza!

2. Look at my picture. I just drew a cake!

3. Look at my picture. I just drew a monster!

4. Look at my picture. The monster just ate the pizza and cake!

WRITE!

1. What three things does the boy draw?

_____
_____
_____
_____
_____

2. Is this story real or pretend? How do you know?

_____
_____
_____
_____
_____

SHADE!

1. The boy in the story draws pictures.

TRUE   FALSE

2. The boy in the story reads books.

TRUE   FALSE

DRAW!

Who ate the pizza and cake?

We Love to Play Soccer

1

I am Pam.
I love to play soccer.
See me run!

2

I am Sam.
I love to play soccer.
See me kick!

3

I am Tam.
I love to play soccer.
See me score!

4

We are Pam and
Sam and Tam.
We love to play soccer.
See us cheer!

First Comprehension: Comics © Scholastic Inc.

WRITE!

1. What game do the kids love to play?

_____

- -

_____

- -

_____

2. Why do the kids cheer at the end of the story?

_____

- -

_____

- -

_____

SHADE!

1. A boy named Tom is playing soccer.

(TRUE)   (FALSE)

2. A girl named Pam is playing soccer.

(TRUE)   (FALSE)

DRAW!

What does Tam do with the ball?

First Comprehension: Comics © Scholastic Inc.

I Will Share

I am Bill.
I will share my sandwich
with my buddy, Jill.

I am Jill.
I will share my book
with my buddy, Gill.

I am Gill.
I will share my markers
with my buddies,
Bill and Jill.

We are Bill
and Jill and Gill.
Look what we made
together!

First Comprehension: Comics © Scholastic Inc.

Name: _____

WRITE!

1. What are the names of the kids in the story?

_____

_____

_____

_____

2. What do all the kids make together?

_____

_____

_____

_____

SHADE!

1. Bill shares his cookie with Jill.

(TRUE)   (FALSE)

2. Bill shares his sandwich with Jill.

(TRUE)   (FALSE)

DRAW!

What does Jill share with Gill?

Silly Spaghetti

1

2

3

4

First Comprehension: Comics © Scholastic Inc.

WRITE!

1. What food does Kim like to eat?

_____
_____
_____
_____

2. What is silly about Kim's spaghetti?

_____
_____
_____
_____

SHADE!

1. Kim puts candy on her spaghetti.

TRUE   FALSE

2. Kim puts cupcakes on her spaghetti.

TRUE   FALSE

DRAW!

What would you put on your silly spaghetti?

The Shape Snake

1

2

3

4

WRITE!

1. What is the FIRST shape the snake makes?

_____

- -

_____

_____

- -

_____

2. Why do you think the snake makes a heart shape?

_____

- -

_____

_____

- -

_____

SHADE!

1. The animals in this story are frogs.

(TRUE)   (FALSE)

2. The animals in this story are snakes.

(TRUE)   (FALSE)

DRAW!

What shape does the snake make when he sees the tent?

Mouse Buys Balloons

First Comprehension Comics © Scholastic Inc.

Name: _____

WRITE!

1. What did the mouse buy?

_____

_____

_____

_____

2. What happened at the end of the story?

_____

_____

_____

_____

SHADE!

1. A mouse bought balloons.

   TRUE   FALSE

2. A bug bought balloons.

   TRUE   FALSE

DRAW!

How many balloons did the mouse buy?

Super Frog

1

I am Super Frog! Watch me swim.

2

I am Super Frog! Watch me hop.

3

I am Super Frog! Watch me kick.

4

I am Super Frog! Watch me save the day.

WRITE!

1. What is the FIRST thing Super Frog does?

_____

- -

_____

- -

_____

2. How does Super Frog save the day?

_____

_____

_____

- -

_____

SHADE!

1. A bird is the robber.

(TRUE)   (FALSE)

2. A bug is the robber.

(TRUE)   (FALSE)

DRAW!

What else might Super Frog be able to do?

The Best Nest

1 Is a garden the best place for me to build a nest? No, no, no!

2 Is a pond the best place for me to build a nest? No, no, no!

3 Is a cave the best place for me to build a nest? No, no, no!

4 Is a tree the best place for me to build a nest? Yes, yes, yes!

Name: _____

WRITE!

1. What does this bird want to find?

_____

- -

_____

_____

- -

_____

2. How does the story end?

_____

- -

_____

_____

- -

_____

SHADE!

1. The bird flies in this story.

(TRUE)   (FALSE)

2. The bird walks in this story.

(TRUE)   (FALSE)

DRAW!

What does the bird lay in her nest?

33

Olive the Octopus

1

2

3

4

WRITE!

1. What kind of animal is Olive?

_____

_____

_____

_____

2. What happens at the end of the story? Why?

_____

_____

_____

_____

SHADE!

1. Olive cooks soup in the story.

TRUE   FALSE

2. Olive reads books in the story.

TRUE   FALSE

DRAW!

What else can this octopus do?

The Cat's Hat

1

2

3

4

Name: _____

The Cat's Hat

WRITE!

1. What is the cat's name?

_____

_____

_____

_____

2. What does the cat like to wear?

_____

_____

_____

_____

SHADE!

1. The cat says, "Meow!"

TRUE   FALSE

2. The cat says, "Bow-wow!"

TRUE   FALSE

DRAW!

Who took the cat's hat?

37

Dot With Spots

1

Bow-wow! My name is Dot. I have lots and lots of spots.

2

My bone has lots and lots of spots. So does my bowl.

3

My ball has lots and lots of spots. So does my bear.

4

My bed has lots and lots of spots. It is a great place to hide!

WRITE!

1. What does Dot have lots and lots of?

_____

- -

_____

_____

- -

_____

2. Where does Dot hide?

_____

- -

_____

_____

- -

_____

SHADE!

1. Dot is a cat with spots.

TRUE   FALSE

2. Dot is dog with spots.

TRUE   FALSE

DRAW!

What spotted things does
Dot have?

39

Penguin Pals

1

Hi! Our names are Sal and Val. We are your penguin pals. We love winter!

2

We love winter because we can sled down this hill. Slide, slide!

3

We love winter because we can skate on this lake. Glide, glide!

4

We love winter because we can drink this hot chocolate. Yum, yum!

WRITE!

1. What are the names of the two penguins?

_____

- -

_____

_____

- -

_____

2. What season do the penguin pals love? Why?

_____

- -

_____

_____

- -

_____

SHADE!

1. The penguins skate in the story.

(TRUE)   (FALSE)

2. The penguins sleep in the story.

(TRUE)   (FALSE)

DRAW!

What else do the penguins do?

The Tiny Elephant

1

Hello! My name is Ed.
I'm an elephant and
I am very, very tiny.

2

I like puddles.
I jump in and swim.
Splash, splash!

3

I like peanuts.
I eat one for dinner.
Yum, yum!

4

I do NOT like mice.
I run from them.
Bye-bye!

Name: _____

WRITE!

1. How is Ed different from other elephants?

_____

- -

_____

- -

_____

2. What happens at the end of the story?

_____

- -

_____

- -

_____

SHADE!

1. Ed swims in a puddle.

TRUE   FALSE

2. Ed swims in a tub.

TRUE   FALSE

DRAW!

What does Ed eat for dinner?

I Am Afraid

1

2

3

4

WRITE!

1. What things is this monster afraid of?

_____
_____
_____
_____

2. What thing is the monster NOT afraid of?

_____
_____
_____
_____

SHADE!

1. This story is about a ghost.

(TRUE) (FALSE)

2. This story is about a monster.

(TRUE) (FALSE)

DRAW!

What else might the monster be afraid of?

Two Boots

1 We are two boots. We walk and walk!

2 We are two boots. We talk and talk!

Hello! Hello!

3 We are two boots. We hop and hop!

4 We are two boots. We bop and bop!

Name: _____

WRITE!

1. What is the FIRST thing the two boots do?

_____
- -
_____
_____
- -
_____

2. Is this story real or pretend? How do you know?

_____
- -
_____
_____
- -
_____

SHADE!

1. The two boots hop.

(TRUE)   (FALSE)

2. The two boots eat.

(TRUE)   (FALSE)

DRAW!

What else do you think these two boots could do?

47

Robot Farm

WRITE!

1. What four animals are on the Robot Farm?

_____

- -

_____

_____

- -

_____

2. What do the animals do when the rooster crows? Why?

_____

- -

_____

_____

- -

_____

SHADE!

1. The robot cow says BEEP OINK!

TRUE   FALSE

2. The robot cow says BEEP MOO!

TRUE   FALSE

DRAW!

What other animal might live on the Robot Farm. What would it say?

Bill the Giant

WRITE!

1. Is Bill real or pretend? How do you know?

_____

- -

_____

_____

- -

_____

2. What is Bill taller than?

_____

- -

_____

_____

- -

_____

SHADE!

1. Bill is a giant.

TRUE   FALSE

2. Bill is an elf.

TRUE   FALSE

DRAW!

Who is taller than Bill?

The Snow Boy

1

2

3

4

Name: _____

WRITE!

1. Who is the main character of this story?

_____
- -
_____
_____
- -
_____

2. Where does the snow boy go?

_____
- -
_____
_____
- -
_____

SHADE!

1. The snow boy eats ice cream.

TRUE   FALSE

2. The snow boy builds a snow
tower.

TRUE   FALSE

DRAW!

What happens at the end of
the story?

First Comprehension: Comics © Scholastic Inc.

53

The Ice Cream Cone

1

Hi there!
I am an ice cream cone.
I have three big scoops.

2

I like the snow.
It is cold, cold, cold!
I play with my pal.

3

I like the freezer.
It is cold, cold, cold!
I read a book.

4

I do NOT like the beach.
It is hot, hot, hot!
Oh, no!

WRITE!

1. Does the ice cream cone like snow? Why?

_____
_____
_____
_____

2. At the end of the story, why does the ice cream cone say, "Oh, no!"

_____
_____
_____
_____

SHADE!

1. The ice cream cone likes the beach.

TRUE   FALSE

2. The ice cream cone does NOT like the beach.

TRUE   FALSE

DRAW!

How many scoops does the ice cream cone have?

Spider Notes

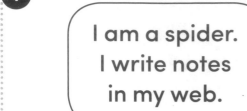

First Comprehension: Comics © Scholastic Inc.

WRITE!

1. What does this spider do that is special?

_____

- -

_____

_____

- -

_____

2. This spider wants to be pals with someone. Who?

_____

- -

_____

_____

- -

_____

SHADE!

1. The spider writes a note about a tree.

TRUE   FALSE

2. The spider writes a note about a rose.

TRUE   FALSE

DRAW!

What note would you write to this spider?

I Love to Skate

1

I am a rabbit named Ray.
I love to skate
with pizza on a tray.

2

I am a rabbit named Ray.
I love to skate with pizza
and cake on a tray.

3

I am a rabbit named Ray.
I slipped.
Down go my tray and
pizza and cake!

4

I am a rabbit named Ray.
I learned my lesson.
Now I skate with a table.

Name: _____

WRITE!

1. What happened when Ray slipped?

_____

_____

_____

_____

2. How did Ray solve his problem?

_____

_____

_____

_____

SHADE!

1. Ray the Rabbit loves to skate.

TRUE FALSE

2. Ray the Rabbit loves to swim.

TRUE FALSE

DRAW!

What was on Ray's tray?

Answer Key

Name: Tara S.   I Dress Up

WRITE!

1. What does the girl dress up as FIRST?

The first thing the girl
dresses up as is a clown.

2. What insect does the girl dress up as?

The girl dresses up
as a bee.

SHADE!

1. The girl dresses up as a cat.

(TRUE)   (FALSE)

2. The girl dresses up as a dinosaur.

(TRUE)   FALSE

DRAW!

What do you like to dress up as?

Answers will vary.

11

Name: Tara S.   Big Surprise

WRITE!

1. What do the friends bring to the party?

They bring a balloon,
a present, and a cake.

2. What happens at the end of the story?

The girl has a surprise
party!

SHADE!

1. One friend has a cake.

(TRUE)   FALSE

2. One friend has a flower.

TRUE   (FALSE)

DRAW!

How old is the girl? Draw a cake with that many candles.

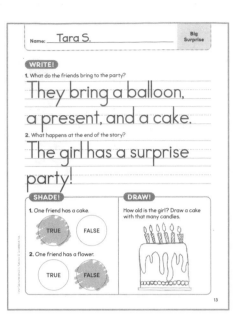

13

Name: Tara S.   Baby's Socks

WRITE!

1. What is Baby playing with?

Baby is playing with
his socks.

2. Is Baby silly? Why?

Yes. Baby is silly because
he puts his socks on his ears!

SHADE!

1. Baby is young.

(TRUE)   FALSE

2. Baby is old.

TRUE   (FALSE)

DRAW!

Where does Baby put his socks at the end of the story?

15

Name: Tara S.   Hide-and-Seek Mouse

WRITE!

1. What game are the mouse and boy playing?

They are playing hide
and seek.

2. What is the FIRST place the mouse hides?

The first place the mouse
hides is in the box.

SHADE!

1. The mouse hides in a bag.

TRUE   (FALSE)

2. The mouse hides in a mug.

(TRUE)   FALSE

DRAW!

What place does the mouse NOT get found?

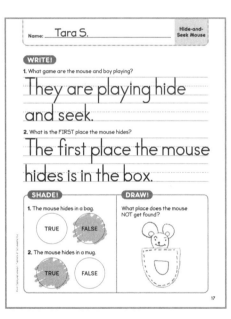

17

Name: Tara S.   My Picture

WRITE!

1. What three things does the boy draw?

The boy draws a pizza,
a cake, and a monster.

2. Is this story real or pretend? How do you know?

The story is pretend because a picture
of a monster could not eat food!

SHADE!

1. The boy in the story draws pictures.

(TRUE)   FALSE

2. The boy in the story reads books.

TRUE   (FALSE)

DRAW!

Who ate the pizza and cake?

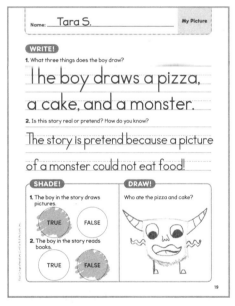

19

Name: Tara S.   We Love to Play Soccer

WRITE!

1. What game do the kids love to play?

The kids love to play
soccer.

2. Why do the kids cheer at the end of the story?

They cheer because
Tam makes a goal.

SHADE!

1. A boy named Tom is playing soccer.

TRUE   (FALSE)

2. A girl named Pam is playing soccer.

(TRUE)   FALSE

DRAW!

What does Tam do with the ball?

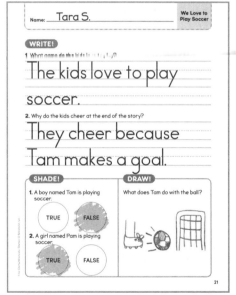

21

Name: Tara S.   I Will Share

WRITE!

1. What are the names of the kids in the story?

The names of the kids
are Bill and Jill and Gill.

2. What do all the kids make together?

They make a poster that says,
WE LOVE TO SHARE!

SHADE!

1. Bill shares his cookie with Jill.

TRUE   (FALSE)

2. Bill shares his sandwich with Jill.

(TRUE)   FALSE

DRAW!

What does Jill share with Gill?

23

Name: Tara S.   Silly Spaghetti

WRITE!

1. What food does Kim like to eat?

Kim likes to eat silly
spaghetti.

2. What is silly about Kim's spaghetti?

The spaghetti is silly because
it has stinky cheese on it!

SHADE!

1. Kim puts candy on her spaghetti.

TRUE   (FALSE)

2. Kim puts cupcakes on her spaghetti.

(TRUE)   FALSE

DRAW!

What would you put on your silly spaghetti?

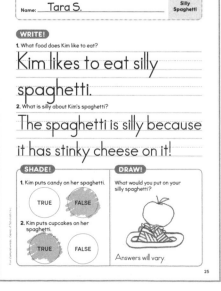

Answers will vary.

25

Name: Tara S.   The Shape Snake

WRITE!

1. What is the FIRST shape the snake makes?

The first shape the
snake makes is a circle.

2. Why do you think the snake makes a heart shape?

The snake makes a heart because
he loves the snake he sees.

SHADE!

1. The animals in this story are frogs.

TRUE   (FALSE)

2. The animals in this story are snakes.

(TRUE)   FALSE

DRAW!

What shape does the snake make when he sees the tent?

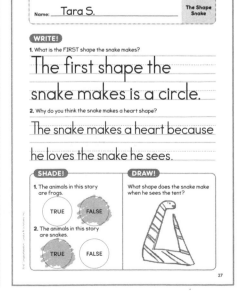

27

60

First Comprehension Comics © Scholastic Inc.

Answer Key

Name: **Tara S.** | Mouse Buys Balloons

WRITE!

1. What did the mouse buy?

The mouse bought balloons.

2. What happened at the end of the story?

The mouse floated up in the air!

SHADE!

1. A mouse bought balloons.
TRUE FALSE

2. A bug bought balloons.
TRUE FALSE

DRAW!

How many balloons did the mouse buy?

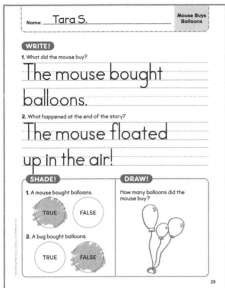

29

Name: **Tara S.** | Super Frog

WRITE!

1. What is the FIRST thing Super Frog does?

The first thing Super Frog does is swim.

2. How does Super Frog save the day?

He kicks the bad bug and gets the money.

SHADE!

1. A bird is the robber.
TRUE FALSE

2. A bug is the robber.
TRUE FALSE

DRAW!

What else might Super Frog be able to do?

Answers will vary.

31

Name: **Tara S.** | The Best Nest

WRITE!

1. What does this bird want to find?

The bird wants to find the best place to build a nest.

2. How does the story end?

The bird finds a tree and builds a nest there.

SHADE!

1. The bird flies in this story.
TRUE FALSE

2. The bird walks in this story.
TRUE FALSE

DRAW!

What does the bird lay in her nest?

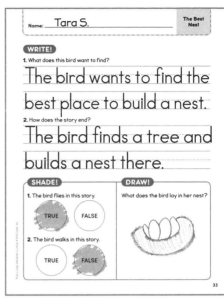

33

Name: **Tara S.** | Olive the Octopus

WRITE!

1. What kind of animal is Olive?

Olive is an octopus.

2. What happens at the end of the story? Why?

Olive makes a big mess when she does too many things.

SHADE!

1. Olive cooks soup in the story.
TRUE FALSE

2. Olive reads books in the story.
TRUE FALSE

DRAW!

What else can this octopus do?

35

Name: **Tara S.** | The Cat's Hat

WRITE!

1. What is the cat's name?

The cat's name is Tad.

2. What does the cat like to wear?

The cat likes to wear a silly hat.

SHADE!

1. The cat says, "Meow!"
TRUE FALSE

2. The cat says, "Bow-wow!"
TRUE FALSE

DRAW!

Who took the cat's hat?

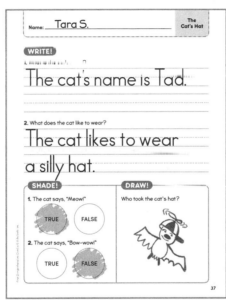

37

Name: **Tara S.** | Dot With Spots

WRITE!

1. What does Dot have lots and lots of?

Dot has lots and lots of spots!

2. Where does Dot hide?

Dot hides in the dog bed.

SHADE!

1. Dot is a cat with spots.
TRUE FALSE

2. Dot is dog with spots.
TRUE FALSE

DRAW!

What spotted things does Dot have?

39

Name: **Tara S.** | Penguin Pals

WRITE!

1. What are the names of the two penguins?

Their names are Sal and Val.

2. What season do the penguin pals love? Why?

The penguins love winter because they can sled.

SHADE!

1. The penguins skate in the story.
TRUE FALSE

2. The penguins sleep in the story.
TRUE FALSE

DRAW!

What else do the penguins do?

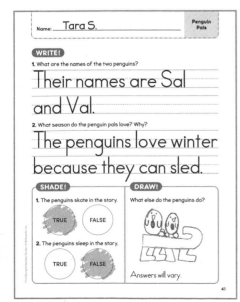

Answers will vary.

41

Name: **Tara S.** | The Tiny Elephant

WRITE!

1. How is Ed different from other elephants?

Ed is different from other elephants because he is tiny.

2. What happens at the end of the story?

At the end of the story, Ed runs away from mice.

SHADE!

1. Ed swims in a puddle.
TRUE FALSE

2. Ed swims in a tub.
TRUE FALSE

DRAW!

What does Ed eat for dinner?

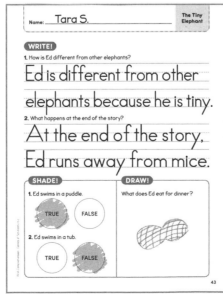

43

Name: **Tara S.** | I Am Afraid

WRITE!

1. What things is this monster afraid of?

The monster is afraid of bats and bugs and snakes.

2. What thing is the monster NOT afraid of?

The monster is not afraid of monsters!

SHADE!

1. This story is about a ghost.
TRUE FALSE

2. This story is about a monster.
TRUE FALSE

DRAW!

What else might the monster be afraid of?

Answers will vary.

45

Answer Key

Name: Tara S.   Two Boots

WRITE!

1. What is the FIRST thing the two boots do?

The first thing the boots do is walk.

2. Is this story real or pretend? How do you know?

This story is pretend because boots can't talk and dance!

SHADE!

1. The two boots hop.
TRUE **FALSE**

2. The two boots eat.
TRUE **FALSE**

DRAW!

What else do you think these two boots could do?

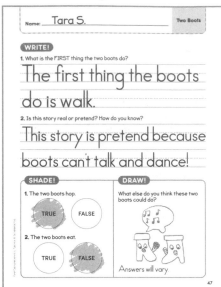

Answers will vary.

47

Name: Tara S.   Robot Farm

WRITE!

1. What four animals are on the Robot Farm?

The four animals on the farm are a cow, pig, sheep, and rooster.

2. What do the animals do when the rooster crows? Why?

They cover their ears because the rooster is loud!

SHADE!

1. The robot cow says BEEP OINK!
TRUE **FALSE**

2. The robot cow says BEEP MOO!
TRUE FALSE

DRAW!

What other animal might live on the Robot Farm. What would it say?

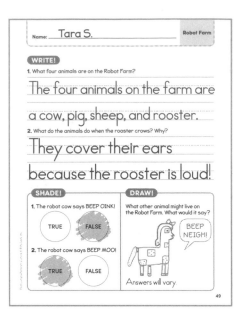

BEEP NEIGH!

Answers will vary.

49

Name: Tara S.   Bill the Giant

WRITE!

1. Is Bill real or pretend? How do you know?

Bill is pretend because he is too tall to be real.

2. What is Bill taller than?

Bill is taller than a tree, a house, and a hill.

SHADE!

1. Bill is a giant.
TRUE FALSE

2. Bill is an elf.
TRUE **FALSE**

DRAW!

Who is taller than Bill?

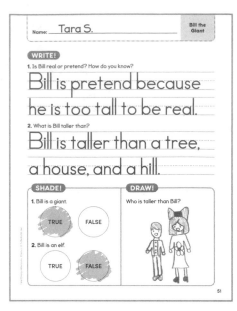

51

Name: Tara S.   The Snow Boy

WRITE!

1. Who is the main character of this story?

The main character is a snow boy.

2. Where does the snow boy go?

The snow boy goes to snow school.

SHADE!

1. The snow boy eats ice cream.
TRUE **FALSE**

2. The snow boy builds a snow tower.
TRUE FALSE

DRAW!

What happens at the end of the story?

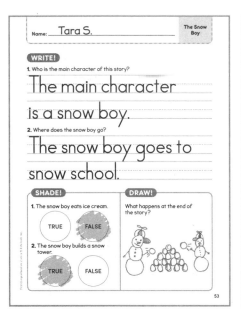

53

Name: Tara S.   The Ice Cream Cone

WRITE!

1. Does the ice cream cone like snow? Why?

The ice cream cone likes snow because it is cold.

2. At the end of the story, why does the ice cream cone say, "Oh, no!"

The ice cream cone says, "Oh, no!" because he does not want to melt.

SHADE!

1. The ice cream cone likes the beach.
TRUE **FALSE**

2. The ice cream cone does NOT like the beach.
TRUE FALSE

DRAW!

How many scoops does the ice cream cone have?

55

Name: Tara S.   Spider Notes

WRITE!

1. What does this spider do that is special?

He writes notes in his web.

2. This spider wants to be pals with someone. Who?

He wants to be pals with me!

SHADE!

1. The spider writes a note about a tree.
TRUE **FALSE**

2. The spider writes a note about a rose.
TRUE FALSE

DRAW!

What note would you write to this spider?

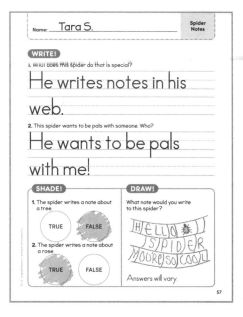

HELLO SPIDER YOU ARE SO COOL

Answers will vary.

57

Name: Tara S.   I Love to Skate

WRITE!

1. What happened when Ray slipped?

When Ray slipped, he dropped his tray of food.

2. How did Ray solve his problem?

Ray solved his problem by skating with a table.

SHADE!

1. Ray the Rabbit loves to skate.
TRUE FALSE

2. Ray the Rabbit loves to swim.
TRUE **FALSE**

DRAW!

What was on Ray's tray?

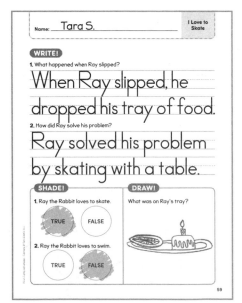

59

Notes

Notes